GREAT-GRANDPA, TELL ME YOUR LIFE STORY

A guided journal filled with questions for great-grandfathers to answer for their great-grandchildren.

Great-Grandpa, Tell Me Your Life Story

Copyright © 2019 by Jean Lee

Cover Design by Jean Lee

All rights reserved. No part of this book may be reproduced without written permission of the copyright owner, except for the use of limited quotations for the purpose of book reviews.

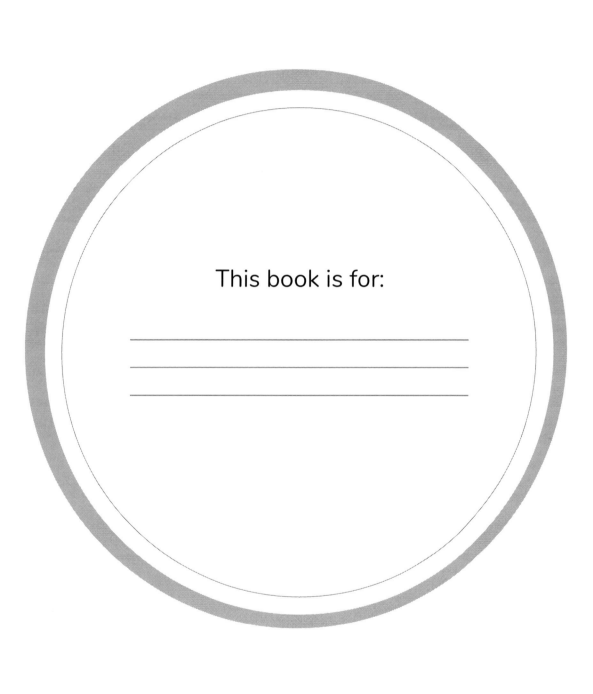

This book is for:

_____
_____
_____

DATE:

What is your full name and birthday? Where were you born (city, state, and hospital)? Do you know your birth stats (time, weight, height)? Any interesting stories you've been told about the day you were born?

DATE:

What were your parent's full names and birthdays?
Where were your parents born?
If your parents have passed, what dates did they die on and what were the causes of their deaths?

DATE:

What are the names and birthdays of your siblings?
Where do you fall in the birth order?
Which sibling were you closest to growing up?
What did you play with together as kids?

DATE: _____

Tell me about your favorite grandparents, aunts, uncles, or cousins? Are they still living? Do you have any special memories of time spent with them?

DATE:

Did you know your great-grandparents? Tell me anything special about our relatives, including their military service, unique talents, or special jobs they may have had.

DATE:

What were the names of the schools you attended and what cities were they in? Did you graduate from high school? College?

DATE:

What were your favorite subjects in school?
Which subjects did you hate?
What were your grades like?

DATE:

What were you like a child?
What were your hobbies and interests?
What did you do for fun?

DATE: _____

Did you participate in any activities such as sports or music? Did you attend the school dances? Were you in any plays or concerts?

_____
_____
_____
_____
_____
_____
_____
_____
_____
_____
_____
_____
_____
_____

DATE:

What is your best memory from childhood?
What is your worst? Would you say you had a good childhood or a bad one?

DATE:

List all of the jobs you've had throughout your life. Which was your favorite? Which was your least favorite? Do you remember how much money you made at each?

DATE:

What was your first car? Do you remember how much you paid for it? What was the best car you've had in your life? Which was the worst? What is your dream car?

DATE:

Tell me about how you met my great-grandma.
Where did you go on your first date?
What qualities attracted you to her?

DATE:

How did you and my great-grandma become engaged?
Did you have bachelor and bachelorette parties?
Any special story behind your rings?

DATE:

What was your wedding like?
Who was in your wedding party?
What was the song for your first dance?
Did you go on a honeymoon?

DATE:

Tell me about all of the homes you've lived in.
Which was your favorite? Which one was the worst?
Describe your dream home.

DATE:

Tell me what life was like for you in your 20's.
What were you like? What were your hobbies and interests?
Were you happy?

DATE:

Tell me what life was like for you in your 30's.
What were you like? What were your hobbies and interests? Were you happy?

DATE:

Tell me what life was like for you in your 40's.
What were you like? What were your hobbies and interests? Were you happy?

DATE:

What were your favorite foods growing up?
What food do you like best now? What foods do you hate? What is the best meal you've ever had?
What is your favorite restaurant?

DATE:

What was your favorite type of music growing up?
What is your favorite song of all time?
Who is your favorite singer or band of all time?
Have you been to any concerts?

DATE:

Do you enjoy reading?
What authors and/or books are your favorites?
Do you like to read newspapers and/or magazines?
If so, which titles?

DATE: _____

What were your favorite radio and/or television shows growing up? Which are your all-time favorites? Who is your favorite TV actor or actress? What is your current favorite television show?

_____
_____
_____
_____
_____
_____
_____
_____
_____
_____
_____
_____
_____
_____
_____
_____

DATE:

Do you like to watch sports?
If so, what sports do you enjoy?
Which teams are your favorite?
Who is your favorite athlete?
Have you ever attended a game in person?

DATE:

Tell me about your favorites.
Favorite color? Favorite season?
Favorite time of day? Favorite ice cream flavor?
Favorite number? Favorite flower?

DATE:

What is your proudest accomplishment in life?
What is your biggest regret? If you could go back in time and change anything, what would it be?

DATE:

Do you like animals?
Tell me about all of the pets you've had.
Do you prefer dogs or cats?

DATE:

Tell me about any memorable birthdays you've had.
What is the best birthday gift you've ever been given?
What flavor of birthday cake is your favorite?

DATE: _____

Did you serve in the military?
Is so, when and what branch?
Did you serve overseas? Did you see battle?
Did you receive any medals?
Who was your best military buddy?

DATE:

Did you attend church growing up?
Were you baptized?
What religion do you identify with today?

DATE:

What was your most memorable Christmas?
What is the best present you've ever received?
What is the best present you've ever given?

DATE:

Have you taken a lot of vacations during your life? What was the best vacation you've ever been on? The worst? Where would you still like to travel to?

DATE:

List all of the states you've visited.
List all of the countries you've been to.
Is there anywhere you'd like to visit that
you haven't been to yet?

DATE:

Do you remember what you wanted to be when you grew up? Do you wish you had pursued a different career?

DATE:

Tell me about your health.
Do you remember being sick as a child?
What health problems are you facing today?

DATE:

> Have you ever ridden a train?
> Flown in an airplane?
> Been in a boat or on a helicopter?
> Which did you prefer?

DATE: _____

What items have you collected over the years?
Do you still have your collections?
Are you collecting anything these days?

DATE:

What is your idea of the perfect day?
Where would you go? What would the weather be like? What would you eat? Who would be with you?

DATE:

What was the best day of your life?
What was the worst day of your life?

DATE:

How would you like people to remember you?
What would you like to be known for?

DATE:

What traditions have you passed on
to your family that you got from your parents?
What traditions have you given up?

DATE:

What is the most significant world event that you've lived through? Has it had a lasting impact of your life?

DATE:

Do you have any bad habits that you wish you could break? Have people told you that you have a bad habit that you don't believe you actually have?

DATE:

Do you like to go shopping?
What is your favorite store?
What types of things do you hate to shop for?

DATE:

Do you like to cook or bake?
Any special dishes that you love to prepare?

DATE:

Have you ever been camping?
Have you ever ridden a horse?
Swam in a lake or in the ocean?

DATE:

Have you ever met anyone famous
or had a close brush with a celebrity?

DATE:

What is your biggest fear?
Are there fears you had when you
were younger that you've overcome?

DATE:

What rules did you have to follow as a child?
Did you change any of these for raising your own kids?

DATE:

What is your most embarrassing memory as a child?
What is the most embarrassing
thing you've experienced as an adult?

DATE:

What was your most prized childhood possession?
Do you still have it?
What is your most prized possession today?

DATE:

What political party to you belong to?
How many Presidents have you voted for?

DATE:

Do you remember any Christmas presents
you received as a child?
Did you have a Christmas stocking?
If so, what kinds of things were in it?

DATE: _____

What Christmas traditions from your childhood
did you carry over for your own children?

DATE: _____

Which is your favorite season:
Winter, Spring, Summer, or Fall?
Which is your least favorite?
Do you prefer warm or cold weather?

DATE:

How did you spend Thanksgiving as a child?
What traditions have you carried over to your family?
As for turkey, do you prefer white or dark meat?

DATE:

Did you have a role model or mentor growing up?
Did you have any favorite teachers or coaches?

DATE:

Do you remember having nightmares as a child?
Do you have them as an adult?
Have you ever had any recurring dreams?

DATE:

Are you superstitious, such as not letting a black cat cross your path, not walking under ladders, not breaking a mirror, or throwing salt over your shoulder? Do you have a lucky number? A lucky charm?

DATE:

Have you ever been through a natural disaster such as a flood, tornado, or earthquake? Have you ever experienced an excessive heat wave or a massive snow storm? Do you like thunderstorms?

DATE: _____

What was Valentine's Day like when you were a child? What has been your favorite Valentine's Day as an adult?

DATE:

Do you keep in touch with any of your childhood friends?
Have you attended any class reunions?
If you did, were they fun? If you didn't go, why not?

DATE:

What chores did you have as a child?
Did you receive an allowance?

DATE:

Have you had your wisdom teeth removed?
How about your appendix? Tonsils?
What surgeries have you had?

DATE: _____

How did your family celebrate Easter when you were a child? Did you dye and hunt for eggs? Did the Easter bunny come to your house? Did you get an Easter basket?

DATE:

What was your favorite piece of playground equipment as a child? Did you have a fort or secret hiding place?

DATE:

Did you have any nicknames growing up?
Were you ever teased or picked on in school?

DATE:

How did you spend your summers as a child?
Any family vacation traditions?

DATE:

Have you ever been ice skating?
Roller skating? Skiing?
Do you know how to swim?

DATE:

What is the most trouble you ever got into as a child?
What punishments did your parents hand out to you?
Did you ever get in trouble at a job?

DATE:

Have you ever been in a physical fight?
What's the worst argument you've ever had with someone?

DATE:

> Did you go to the school dances in junior high and high school? What about the football and basketball games?

DATE: _____

What was Halloween like when you were a child?
Did you go trick-or-treating?
Do you remember any of the costumes you wore?

DATE:

What were your favorite candies as a child? Do you remember where you bought candy and how much it was? Did you prefer chocolate or non-chocolate sweets?
What is your favorite candy now?

DATE: _____

> Do you have a favorite boss? A boss you couldn't stand? Did you get along with your co-workers? Was there someone you worked with who you really disliked?

_____
_____
_____
_____
_____
_____
_____
_____
_____
_____
_____
_____
_____
_____
_____

DATE:

What is the best part of being a great-grandpa? The hardest? What are your hopes and dreams for your great-grandchildren?

DATE:

What has been your greatest achievement in life?
What has been your biggest regret?

DATE:

How did you choose the names of your children? Were there any alternate names you had in mind?

DATE:

Do you like your name? If you could change your name to anything else, what would it be? What nicknames have you had over the years?

DATE:

What's the best piece of advice you've ever been given? What advice do you wish you would have taken?

DATE: _____

How do you want to spend the last years of your life? Do you want to live where you currently do or someplace else?

_____
_____
_____
_____
_____
_____
_____
_____
_____
_____
_____
_____
_____
_____

DATE:

Do you have any goals and dreams you still want to fulfill?

DATE:

What is your greatest wish for your family?
What is your greatest wish for all of mankind?

DATE:

Do you believe in an afterlife?
Is so, what do you imagine it to be like?

DATE: _____

Did you like answering these questions?
Is there anything else you'd like to tell me?

PHOTOGRAPHS & MEMORABILIA

PHOTOGRAPHS & MEMORABILIA

PHOTOGRAPHS & MEMORABILIA

PHOTOGRAPHS & MEMORABILIA

PHOTOGRAPHS & MEMORABILIA

PHOTOGRAPHS & MEMORABILIA

PHOTOGRAPHS & MEMORABILIA

PHOTOGRAPHS & MEMORABILIA

PHOTOGRAPHS & MEMORABILIA

Made in United States
Troutdale, OR
10/26/2024